*Then their eyes were opened
and they recognized him . . .*
— Luke 24:31

Publisher's Note:

Lo-Ann and David Trembley bring us an extraordinarily timely message on the importance of inclusion that is worthy of the attention of every thoughtful messenger of the Gospel.

Today, with the decline in literacy and the rising number of mentally challenged individuals in our population, due to a variety of environmental, genetic, educational and other causes, the need to explore new ways of communicating the Gospel has become even more urgent.

In fact, the National Adult Literacy Survey revealed that one-fourth (40-44 million) of the adults living in the United States in 1992 demonstrated literacy skills on the very lowest level of proficiency and another 50 million adults demonstrated skills on a level only slightly higher.

Against this alarming trend, *Emmaus Eyes* brings fresh insights to our appreciation and understanding of the Incarnation—the 'Word made flesh,' Who dwells among us! It is time to examine whether that vital sense of the actual Presence of God in our midst may not be in danger of getting lost in styles of worship which focus almost exclusively on the sermon, to the neglect of other equally important aspects.

David and Lo-Ann Trembley show how easy it is, without compromising the Gospel message, to embrace **all** of God's needy children in the healing message of His redeeming love. We at Eden Publishing encourage you, after reading this important ground-breaking book, to share the Trembley's burden with other pastors and laypeople.

In addition, the authors welcome your comments and suggestions, so please feel free to write them at:
David and Lo-Ann Trembley, Co-Pastors
Broken Walls Christian Community
617 West Washington Street
Milwaukee, WI 53204

Emmaus Eyes

WORSHIP *WITH* THE
Mentally Challenged

Lo-Ann and David Trembley

Published by
 EDEN PUBLISHING

ISBN 1-884898-11-4

Library of Congress Catalog Card Number: 96-085866

Printed in the United States of America.

Published by Eden Publishing
8635 West Sahara Avenue, Suite 459
The Lakes, Nevada 89117.

Acknowledgments
All Scripture quotations are from the The Holy Bible, New International Version, Copyright © 1978, New York International Bible Society, and used by permission of Zondervan Bible Publishers; with the exception of Luke 23:1-49, "At the Place of the Skull," which is taken from the Good News Bible in Today's English Version, Copyright © 1966, 1971, 1976 American Bible Society; reprinted by permission.

No one can fully comprehend the uncreated God with . . . knowledge, but each one, in a different way, can grasp him fully through love.

—*The Cloud of Unknowing* (14th Century)

Emmaus Eyes

Table of Contents

Preface to A Decision

Ever notice how many books about worship are aimed at helping readers do more effectively and efficiently pretty much what they have always done? These are essentially books of instructional technique.

Emmaus Eyes: Worship WITH the Mentally Challenged is much more radical and demanding. It presents as many challenges to persons who do not happen to be mentally challenged as it does to those who do. *Emmaus Eyes* asks for significant, even substantial, change from both worship leaders and the people in the pew, because the book claims that traditional Christian worship has a serious deficiency. It shuts people out from the Kingdom of God.

Harsh words. Why should anyone take them seriously?

The first pieces of evidence come from looking at typical Christian congregations at worship on Sunday morning. With few exceptions, these congregations are just as homogenous as they can be. They are either all white or all Black, all Hispanic or all Anglo, all middle class or all poor (or some other socioeconomic designation).

The homogeneity is easily explained. We human beings like to associate with persons who are like us. Differences make us uncomfortable. It's a simple sociological fact of life that people cross as few barriers as possible on our way to relationship.

Sociology, however, is in considerable tension with Christian faithfulness. "With his own body," Ephesians 2:14

says, "he broke down the wall that separated them and kept them enemies." Galatians 3:28 adds, "So there is no difference between Jews and Gentiles . . . slaves and free . . . men and women; you are all one in union with Christ Jesus."

One might argue that this oneness is either "cosmic" or a hope for that time when the Kingdom of God will arrive in its complete power. Such a claim, however, avoids the central mystery of Christianity, which is the Incarnation. God came to the world, in the Person of Christ Jesus, to a particular place, to a particular people, and at a particular time. One of the fundamental claims of *Emmaus Eyes* is that this particularity is not an accident. Attempting to actually live in union with the wondrously diverse body of Christ is not an optional extra. It is, rather, central to what the reality of Christian discipleship means.

Secondly, there is a clear mandate in Scripture to minister to "the least of these." Matthew 25:31-46 presents the matter most graphically. The concluding verses of that passage read, "I tell you, whenever you refused to help one of these least important ones, you refused to help me. These, then, will be sent off to eternal punishment, but the righteous will go to eternal life" (Matthew 25.45b-46).

There are surely Christians who will think about these issues and decide that they are not as clear as we are claiming. There are all sorts of ways to argue that the Church, as it is currently constituted and behaving, is being faithful enough to the invitation to live and share God's Good News. We are not interested in arguing with persons who decide to commit themselves to maintaining the status quo. Neither are we interested in judging them. But for those who are at least intrigued enough to keep reading, we would like to offer you an invitation to a very exciting adventure indeed.

It turns out that deciding to consciously attempt to cross as many barriers as possible on the way to relationship may not be good sociology, but it is "good Christianity," and it is very enlivening for everyone concerned. The people who can teach us the most are the people who are the most different from us. Seeking out different-ness on purpose is neither a very quick nor a very efficient way to make a church, but it results in a congregation that is filled with excitement and energy.

Since *Emmaus Eyes* talks specifically about including those who happen to be mentally challenged, we shall focus on attempts which invite such persons. It will be helpful for you, however, to keep other populations in mind as you read. What if "the others" you are called to reach out to (and, therefore, are seeking to include) speak a different language, come from an environment very different from your environment, and have very different ideas from yours about who God is and how God is to be worshiped? If you could meet on common ground (not so much compromise as real communion), would not the spiritual journeys of all of you be greatly deepened and stretched?

Many potential changes are neither very radical nor terribly disconcerting. For example, at the time of greeting, one could have the worshipers actually begin to get to know each other rather than simply nod, wave, or smile from their place in the pew. It would mean getting people up on their feet and asking them to move around. It would probably also mean teaching them some basic hospitality procedures—such social skills as making introductions and really listening to what others have to say. Even these little changes might cause some uproar in very staid congregations, but most of us could manage them if we really decided to, and if we did inaugurate these innovations, it would probably be good for everyone concerned.

There is a great range of things we might do to make worship more active and engaging. The potential innovations range from the hardly noticeable to the radically innovative. Ultimately in the process, however, if we are really serious about including persons who happen to be mentally challenged in our worshipping community, we must come to the realization that even the sermon will have to change.

The sermon! Oh, no! Many, perhaps most, pastors cannot imagine what they would do if they were no longer able to preach the sorts of sermons they learned to create in seminary and have been preaching for as many years as they have been ordained.

The problem with traditional sermons, of course, is that they are not, in fact, a very effective means of communication. Professional educators have known for many years that people retain only about twenty percent, at best, of what they hear. If we want real learning, especially in this visual culture in which we now live, we must offer a variety of communicative stimuli.

Even visuals are not enough. The most effective learning, we know, comes when persons are actively engaged in the learning process. Strategies like role play and problem solving increase the amount of learning that is going on to a very marked degree.

There is one additional more or less graceful way to try to escape from the implications of what professional educators have known for generations. One might claim that Christian worship is not really about growing, changing and learning at all. Others might want to say that what worship is supposed to do is comfort folks and "charge their spiritual batteries." We think that these are spurious claims. It seems to us that they completely avoid the facts that most sermons have exhortations and the part of worship termed "response to the Word" includes things like altar calls and invitations to commitment to new ministries.

Of course, if Christian worship is *not* about changed living and changed lives, all sorts of worship styles and practices might be allowed. There might even be room for the "entertainment worship" practiced by some of the more successful mega-churches of recent times.

We believe, however, that the Christian Church ought to be in the vanguard of the new creation which Jesus proclaimed. If that belief is true, then many traditional forms and practices will have to go. Every "piece" of the Sunday morning worship experience will need to be tested by such questions as these: Does this practice promote the growth of Christian disciples? Are these behaviors the sorts of activities which empower persons to be more loving, joyous, peaceful, patient, kind, good, faithful, humble and self-controlled?

It is easy for all concerned, for both pastors and laypeople, to get dismayed by the size of the task we are suggesting. Be sure of one thing. If a congregation decides to begin worshipping in ways which invite a fuller measure of inclusion, participation and empowerment, the pastor will *not* soon be out of a job. The truth is that there is even more to do in designing and conducting active worship than there is in preparing a sermon and fitting it into the traditional forms.

How to begin worshipping in such a fashion is what *Emmaus Eyes* is about. The book does not contain all the answers. Indeed, it is only a suggestive beginning, but we are convinced that churches that actually begin changing will experience such a growth in both numbers and energy that they will wonder why they didn't start this journey years ago.

Threatening? Sure. Challenging? No doubt about it. The fact remains that most folk are not in Christian worship on a typical Sunday morning. They are doing something else with their spirituality that the ordinary Christian congregation has not yet found ways to connect with. Finding these persons and really inviting them into the community, we think, will bring you so much energy and joy that you will be tempted to return to the old forms only on "History Sunday," when you have gathered to honor the memories of where you used to be.

Think about the phrase "Emmaus eyes." Think specifically about when you celebrate Communion during Sunday morning worship. Do the hearts of the worshipers **burn** within them? Do they truly say, "We have **seen** the Lord"? Do you want to get started on the sort of adventure that would able you to answer "yes" to both of those questions?

Part One

As the Body of Christ, twentieth century congregations have come a long way in noticing and responding more appropriately to the physically challenged. Wheelchair lifts and accessible restrooms are at last fairly common in the buildings where we worship. Most of us, however, have not yet even begun to adjust our congregational lives in order to meet the needs of those who happen to be mentally and emotionally challenged.

By the way, we do not say "persons who *are* mentally challenged." Instead, we say "persons who *happen to be* mentally challenged."

The distinction is not merely in grammar.

The message is that mental challenge is not the distinctive characteristic of a person; it is simply one of the characteristics which *happen* to be true.

A few congregations have special services for those who happen to be mentally challenged. These services are often versions of "children's church." Those who happen to be mentally challenged are separated from the "normal" congregation and provided an abbreviated and watered down version of what the rest of us are doing in the sanctuary. In congregations where a separate service is not offered, if mentally challenged persons show up for worship, they are expected to sit quietly for an hour or so and listen to what they cannot possibly understand.

Sitting quietly and listening are not always the behaviors that make for faithful worship. Indeed, attempting to force such behaviors can muffle and stifle the relationship building process and produce worship that is flat, dry, dull and, finally, faithless.

A case in point: At some of the churches Karen attended before coming to Broken Walls, Karen has been told that she must keep still and not make any noise, but Karen has a very lively and enthusiastic faith. She likes to affirm statements about God's love for us with a resounding "Amen!" She purposely brings her Bible to church so she can find appropriate pictures to illustrate whatever is being talked about.

One Sunday Karen was ruffling through her Bible when the Old Testament lesson was Isaiah 66:10-14. She busily flipped through the pages until she found what she was looking for. After the reading (which says, in part, "As a mother comforts her child, so I will comfort you . . . "), Karen held up a picture of the Baby Jesus in the manger.

Thus Karen seriously participated in the reading by not sitting still. Rather than being a distraction, she provided an enriching commentary on the reading. The picture that she lifted up for all to see seemed to convey, "Each of us is a child of God, as precious in God's sight as the Baby in the manger." Karen's activity included us all in this visual insight. As Karen herself would say, "Amen!"

There are surely many theological issues involved in deciding whether or not we are going to work harder to more completely include the mentally challenged in worship and if so how. The main theological issue is one of ecclesiology: What is the Church? We might well change the pronoun and ask: *Who* is the Church?

That's a very big question and certainly worth pondering. A complete answer, however, is beyond the scope of a discussion as modest as this one. In practical terms the decision depends on answers to such questions as these:

◆ Which characteristics of traditional worship are crucial for faithfulness?

◆ Which characteristics are accidents of our time, history and habit?

◆ Who are the mentally challenged?

◆ Does their different ability diminish their humanity, or are they fully human and therefore children of God?

We must all answer these questions for ourselves. After we have answered them, we must then decide what our responsibility is to those who happen to be mentally challenged.

Although the theological issues are important, we believe that most congregations ignore the mentally challenged not from theological reasons but simply out of ignorance and habit. We assume most congregations would welcome in worship those who happen to be mentally challenged if only they knew how to make a winsome invitation.

There is a better way than our old habits. Not worship "for" those who happen to be mentally challenged, but worship "with" them.

That little preposition makes all the difference in the world. The word "with" signals Gospel living. There is no question of superiority or inferiority, of greater or lesser need. When we worship with others, we discover that we are all in the same boat. We are all completely dependent upon the unmerited grace of God.

We achieve the guiding principles for worshipping with those who happen to be mentally challenged by putting **"P-E-P"** into worship. **"P-E-P"** stands for . . .

- ◆ Make it **P**ersonal
- ◆ Make it **E**motional
- ◆ Make it **P**hysical

When worship has **"P-E-P"** it is powerful and effective celebration. The power and faithfulness are magnified for everyone present, not merely (or even mostly) for those who happen to be mentally challenged. Indeed, one of the most surprising benefits of including those who happen to be mentally challenged is the blessing that the newly included bring to the folks who are already there.

Make it Personal

The three parts of **"P-E-P"** are related. In fact, they are three names for the same thing. The opposite of "personal" is "general," and generalizations are the result of analytical thinking. Experiences of joy, happiness and hope are much more than just general concepts. So too, when we are angry, sad, or afraid, we are not necessarily thinking conceptually. In other words, persons have specific experiences that, through a very complex process of making meaning, most of us translate into abstract concepts.

We become attached to our images and ideas. Sooner or later we end up worshipping our images rather than God. That's idolatry. Here's an experiment. Close your eyes and call up your picture of Jesus. Look closely at how *you* see our Savior and Lord.

Did you imagine a flawless Nordic type with flowing blond hair and blue eyes? How does your image square with these words from the prophet Isaiah? "He had no beauty or majesty to attract us to him, nothing in his appearance that we should desire him . . . " (Isaiah 53:2).

The Apostle Paul said, "Now you are the body of Christ, and each one of you is a part of it" (First Corinthians 12:27). If we take these words to heart, worshipping with those who happen to be mentally challenged can help us learn to truly see the face of Christ in others. We will look beyond our images and preconceptions until we are looking "with Emmaus eyes." When our eyes are truly opened, we will recognize Jesus when we see him in spite of missing teeth, trembling hands, stringy greasy hair, faltering gait, or crossed eyes.

Persons who happen to be mentally challenged are not very good at abstract thinking. Nevertheless, they can still participate in and even savor the sorts of experiences that are the basis of such abstractions. Experience and words about experience are not the same. Making worship Personal means providing specific experiences of abstract concepts.

Make It Emotional

As we said, the three parts of **"P-E-P"** are related.

When we worship with those who happen to be mentally challenged, we emotionalize much of what we do. Again, everyone benefits. Many of us have become accustomed to a cold, impersonal, individualistic style of worship. We don't very often cry or laugh freely and certainly not in Sunday morning worship. Shouting our joy and wailing our grief make us equally uncomfortable.

But the Gospel touches us so deeply because it tells stories of people like us shaken by deep feelings. Frightened disciples awaken Jesus shouting "Lord, save us! We're going to drown!" (Matthew 8:25). Jairus throws himself down at Jesus' feet and begs earnestly, "My little daughter is dying. Please come and put your hands on her so that she will be healed and live" (Mark 5:23). A man with an evil spirit comes into the synagogue where Jesus is preaching and screams (Mark 1:23). Jesus himself in Gethsemane says, "My soul is overwhelmed with sorrow to the point of death" (Matthew 26:38).

Throughout the Gospels Jesus encounters and experiences powerful emotions. People come to him with their deepest, truest needs revealed. He receives them and ministers to them. As members of Christ's body in the world, we must learn to deal with honest human emotions, those of others and our own. Worshipping with the mentally challenged can show us how to reclaim a part of our humanity that has been kept out of much of our worship.

Make It Physical

Remember, the three parts of **"P-E-P"** are related.

Making worship physical is a result of the truth that all of the meanings of our lives come to us through our bodies. In its two thousand years of life the Church has often been body-denying, even world-denying. But the Incarnation is the most profound characteristic of Christianity. The Word became *flesh* and dwelt among us. The incredible Christian claim (in the first chapter of First Corinthians Paul calls it "foolishness" and "scandal") is that the God Who made the sun and stars and is the Ruler of the universe became an actual human being.

The Incarnation means that each person is unique and precious to God. Jesus said that when we perform an act of love to "one of the least" it is as though we are doing it to him (Matthew 25:40). So we must find ways in which each person is recognized as special, as a child of God. We are all like common clay pots holding a priceless spiritual treasure (Second Corinthians 4:7). The treasure reveals its value only as we find ways to share it.

We need to make gifts of our treasure. Otherwise it becomes no more than a miser's hoard. ". . . To each one the manifestation of the Spirit is given for the common good" (First Corinthians 12:7). We need to work with the Spirit when we worship with those who happen to be mentally challenged so that all can identify and share the Spirit's gifts.

It is simply not enough to make a few adjustments to meet the needs of those who happen to be mentally challenged. The requirement is much more radical. The radical change will allow the rest of us to experience a dimension of Gospel living that we have been missing.

When we worship with those who happen to be mentally challenged, we must touch each other not only symbolically but *actually* . . . physically. Our physical contact becomes not only an avenue of communication between person and person but also an avenue God's Holy Spirit can use to communicate with each of us individually. Also, folks who happen to be mentally challenged often have a variety of physical difficulties and challenges. Communicating with them physically is a powerful reminder that we, too, live in and have bodies. All of us have limits simply because we are physical creatures in a physical world.

Minnie demonstrates the power of touch better than anyone we know. When it is time for her to get off the bus after worship and return to her room in the residential treatment center where she lives, a simple good-by is never enough for Minnie. Instead, she reaches both arms down to the driver, lays her head on his shoulder and says, "Thank you. I love you. See you soon." Sometimes Minnie adds a light kiss on the cheek. Only then is she satisfied with the adequacy of her good-by. With such spontaneous gestures of physical affection Minnie preaches some of the most powerful sermons we have ever heard.

There is an additional aspect of making worship physical that we must mention. Like all of us, people who happen to be mentally challenged tend to represent value with physical objects. "Kay," for example, is so desperate for something of her own that she sometimes tries to carry away three or four hymnals. When she is reminded, "We'll need those next week," she cheerfully surrenders her loot.

So think about this. You can make worship more meaningful for persons by providing a souvenir of worship to take back home. These objects need not be expensive or elaborate. A Bible, a bright picture, a garment from your congregation's clothing bank, a pen or pencil with the church's name—these are the sorts of simple things that will be treasured.

A P-E-P Quiz

Your congregation is planning a special service. The theme is "Justification by Faith." You have found the perfect responsive reading in your hymnal. You also want to add **"P-E-P"** to your worship. How can you use this responsive reading in ways that include those who happen to be mentally challenged?

Here's the reading:

Leader: Do not bring your servant into judgment, for no one living is righteous before you.

People: **If, in fact, Abraham was justified by works, he had something to boast about.**

Leader: But not before God. What does the Scripture say?

People:	**Abraham believed God, and it was credited to him as righteousness.**
Leader:	Know that a person is not justified by observing the law, but by faith in Jesus Christ.
People:	**So we, too, have put our faith in Christ Jesus that we may be justified by faith in Christ.**
Leader:	And not by observing the law.
People:	**Because by observing the law no one will be justified.**
Leader:	For all have sinned and fall short of the glory of God, and all are justified freely by grace through the redemption that came by Christ Jesus.

[from Psalm 143:2, Romans 4:2-3, Galatians 2:16, and Romans 3:23-24]

What can you do to try to use this reading in a way that includes those who happen to be mentally challenged? Here are three suggestions.

Make it Personal by having different persons read different verses from their various places in the sanctuary. The individual voice tones will allow people to hear the words more clearly, rather than have the message lost in the murmur of a mass reading.

Make the reading Emotional by asking everyone to listen closely during a first reading. Tell them that you will read the passage a second time. When they hear their favorite verse, they should clap or say "Amen."

Make the reading Physical by assigning phrases to small groups. Teach them the phrase. When their turn comes, they should stand (if possible) and recite.

Benefits for the Welcoming Congregation

No doubt there will be resistance to a worship that is more personal, emotional and physical. We will talk in some detail later about how that resistance will show up and how it can best be met. For now, however, let's think about how including persons who happen to be mentally challenged will bring new power and life to your congregation.

Push intellectual abstraction to its limits, and the results are a gassy cloud of vagueness. It is surely true that God is Spirit and Truth, but as Pilate said, "What *is* truth?" When we remain at the abstract level, we are talking about the things of God but not necessarily experiencing them. **So the benefit that comes with welcoming those who happen to be mentally challenged is vibrant worship that is personally addressed to each individual in the congregation.**

Cool, non-emotional worship simply does not meet people where they live. The vast majority of our ordinary life is, in fact, based upon emotion, If our church life is not also basically emotional, it becomes increasing irrelevant and sterile. **So the benefit that comes to the welcoming congregation is worship that is emotionally alive and therefore addressing each person exactly where they live.**

Finally, worship that does not appropriately attend to the fact that all human beings are physical beings leads to additional attempted escapes from reality. If we ignore our bodies, for example, we might more easily ignore the Lord's mandates to feed the hungry and clothe the naked. We will also find it easier to ignore Jesus' special attention to the poor. When we ignore our own bodily nature, we do not see (and, of course, never meet) our own physically based needs. **So the benefit that comes to the welcoming congregation is that all members experience worship as a direct, *physical* source of energy and life.**

Naming the "Pieces" of Worship

Mere tinkering will not do. What is required is a thorough re-examination of what faithful worship is. The first way of meeting that need is naming the "pieces" of worship. As we describe each element, we will ask specifically what our three **"P-E-P"** guidelines require. When this initial discussion is concluded, if you are still a bit vague about how to make actual changes, don't lose heart. Part Two of this book consists of worship services that are created according to the **"P-E-P"** guidelines.

Greeting and Welcome

The sanctuary begins to fill before worship actually begins. Therefore, it is appropriate to give some thought to how persons can be made to feel welcome as soon as they enter the room. Most churches simply pass out the bulletin, an activity usually accompanied by shaking an usher's hand. This routine is a good beginning, but it is possible to offer a much more comprehensive welcome.

In the case of persons who happen to be mentally challenged and have been rejected or excluded from other settings, being made to feel welcome is to experience the Good News. It is particularly an expression of the Gospel's admonition to welcome the outcast and the least of these.

If we want to make personal the idea that worshipers who happen to be mentally challenged are a welcome part of the Christian community, we must find ways to invite their participation and contribution from the time they enter the building. The key insight is that people like to give as well as get. It is not good for us to be always on the receiving end. Especially for folks who are institutionalized, it is very enlivening to be able to make a contribution.

For example, there is always some minor physical preparation to be done. The bulletins need to be folded, or the racks in the pews need to be checked to see that they hold the right numbers and kinds of worship resources. Someone needs to prepare the Lord's Supper, and there may even be some dusting and sweeping to do. Some may need to come to worship a bit early to accomplish these chores, but this little extra effort will build loving relationships and genuine acceptance for persons who happen to be mentally challenged.

Persons who already have worship preparation responsibilities might "adopt" an assistant. The mentors could teach and supervise the task, but the most important thing they do is build relationship by means of recognizing particular persons and their gifts.

People want to share and give of themselves, as Alvin demonstrated one Sunday morning. The night before, he had found out that the van was coming to bring him to church. So Alvin stayed up late drawing pictures and writing page after page. As soon as he was inside the church door, Alvin presented his creation to the pastors. After some careful detective work (because Alvin uses creative spelling, and he would have been insulted if he were told that his gift was unreadable), Alvin's message was decoded to read "Peace be with you."

Alvin's many pages of carefully and laboriously written "Peace be with you" were immediately pinned on the bulletin board in the narthex as an enduring reminder that we all want to give and not just get. We all want to be able to do, make, help and serve in whatever ways we can.

The mundane chores that are a necessity of congregational life become irksome if the same person is always stuck with the same task. Finding someone who takes joy in doing the task can be a wonderful relief.

For example, Dorothy has become the self-selected wastebasket emptier. But she draws the line at carrying the trash out to the dumpster. "I can't do everything," she says. Neither can anyone else do everything, and, of course, we shouldn't try.

Sometimes folks have carved out little niches over the years and guard their responsibilities jealously. We once knew a church usher, for example—surely he wasn't unique—who was so compulsive in discharging his duties that few newcomers could follow all his rules well enough to satisfy him. It was easier for John to do everything himself, and so he did. He shut out a great number of potential contributors to that congregation's life.

The story of Head Usher John offers us all a lesson. It is not only good for the folk who happen to be mentally challenged to undertake the little tasks of hospitality. It is also a breath of fresh air for congregations that have begun to ossify.

Preparing for Worship

The time of coming together affords another way to make worshipers feel welcome and a valued part of the community by insuring whenever possible their familiarity and comfort with the songs, hymns and acts of worship that are going to follow. This transitional time of introduction makes people feel welcome.

The time of greeting and welcome actually belongs to the worship service itself as leader and people greet each other in Christ's name. This is the beginning of the worship service, and beginnings set the tone. First impressions are crucial and determine both our expectations and our kinds and levels of participation. We make this time personal by treating individuals as individuals indeed. We start by sharing names. A simple general greeting from the pulpit will not do. Neither will signing a register in a "ritual of friendship or welcoming of visitors" since many persons who happen to be mentally challenged cannot write their names. Instead, give the worshipers suitable instructions for greeting each other.

Tell them to greet at least three persons by name. This is making the time personal. Suggest that they shake hands (and hug if they want to). This is making the time emotional. Persons might also be invited to tell something that they are happy about. Be sure, however, that everyone is invited to move around in this time of greeting. This is making worship physical.

Depending upon the season or worship theme, alter the instructions for greeting. During Lent, people might share what makes them feel sad or ashamed. In services featuring a major prophet, they might tell what makes them mad. During Holy Week, they might share what makes them feel afraid or hopeful.

This way of greeting is not only good for persons who happen to be mentally challenged. It also is a way of creating community for everyone present—or at least the beginning of community . . . its possibility.

In every congregation there will likely be persons who do not wish to engage in such "intimate" contact. We'll talk more about such persons later. For now, and always, the requirement is to respect them too, in whatever condition they happen to find themselves. Making worship personal, remember, is good for everyone, not only for those who happen to be mentally challenged. Therefore the instructions to greet others are suggestions—and only suggestions, not demands. It is appropriate to say explicitly that the activity is voluntary. Even so, freeing these cold fish up, even a little bit, will be spiritually healthy for them and everyone else.

Music

The music of Christian worship poses a problem for those who happen to be mentally challenged only to the extent that singing requires the ability to read. Three modifi-cations of the traditional way of doing music are possible remedies.

The first possibility is to "line" the songs. Have a strong vocalist sing the line (or simply call out the words). Then the congregation echoes what they have just heard. Given the musical simplicity of much Protestant worship material, it doesn't take long for regular worshipers to know almost by heart many songs.

Lining the music has additional benefits for not only those who happen to be mentally challenged. Now the children will be encouraged to sing, one way in which they too can be included as a vital part of the worshipping community. Also invited in will be those adults who are functionally illiterate. Professional educators say that the functionally illiterate represent anywhere from ten to thirty percent of the general population. There is no need to exclude these non-readers. After all, not too long ago in human history illiteracy was the norm rather than a notable handicap. Often persons who cannot read have developed a very good ear as compensation, so line the songs.

A second possibility is to restrict the music in worship to songs many persons already know. Of course, we do not want to adopt only this strategy because to do so would deprive worshipers of much great music. Nevertheless, there is tremendous emotional power in "Jesus Loves Me," "Jesus Loves the Little Children," "If You're Happy and You Know

It," some of the more familiar Christmas carols and other songs that virtually everyone knows. If you're not already aware of your congregation's favorite hymns, this is a wonderful time to discover them. Choosing those favorites rather than hymns you might think of on your own is a message to persons who are most likely to resist change that they are valued.

Prayer and music can be combined. The "Doxology" and "Gloria" are examples of praying in music that many people already know or can easily learn. Praying the Psalms can be another effective form of call-and-response sung prayer.

A third possibility is perhaps the most surprising. Make up the music. A very simple example is "The Amen Symphony." Take the single word "Amen." Pass it around the congregation. Encourage worshipers to experiment with tone, duration and volume. Everyone sings their "Amen" simultaneously. You might want to cue some of your stronger singers ahead of time, but the precaution is not usually necessary. If the atmosphere is free, reverent, expectant and playful, the music that results can sound in its own way as beautiful as the Mormon Tabernacle Choir.

Once a congregation succeeds with "The Amen Symphony," they may feel ready to try something more adventuresome. Pick a short phrase—for example, "Thank You, Lord God, and Praise You." Divide the congregation into small groups (ten to twenty persons), and have each group set the phrase to music. When you combine all the groups in a call-and-response format, you may be astonished by the worshipful atmosphere that is created.

Two additional ways to make music more emotional and physical are the addition of simple percussion instruments and the use of dance. These choices allow increased participation that does not depend on being skilled with words.

For example, we can enhance the reading of Psalm 65:9-12 with the addition of rainsticks and triangle to imitate the sound of rain dripping its moisture over the wilderness. Similarly, guiro and claves—ask at your local music store—could suggest the "dry parched land" (verse 1) and the desolation (verses 9-11) of Psalm 63.

David's dancing before the Ark (Second Samuel 6:14-15) reveals that dance has a long and honorable tradition in Christian history. The hymns of the Shakers were meant to be danced. These old songs afford a readily available resource for making music more physical and emotional. A piece we now think of as a child's nursery song, "Looby-Loo," was actually sung and danced with appropriate gestures as a Shaker hymn. "I give my [hand, foot . . . self] a shake, shake, shake" represents the shaking off of sin. "I turn myself around" is a sign of turning toward redeemed living.

Naturally, none of these suggestions precludes the presence of special music in worship. When folks are just listening, you can use the same choir anthems, solos and ensemble offerings that you have always included.

"When folks are just listening," we said. These words raise another interesting question. When *should* worshipers be just listening? In what sense is faithful Christian worship a passive activity? To what extent is it appropriate—even necessary—to call for the full, active participation of those in the pew?

The answers to these questions point to the wisdom behind employing anthems that give the whole congregation a familiar or easily learned part to sing or actively involve the people in the anthem by saying "Amen" at its conclusion. If you explain the meaning of "Amen," that it is a Hebrew way of saying, "Yes! That's for me," people are invited to actively listen. At the end of the piece they will "vote" their approval.

Prayer

The invocation, the first prayer of worship, suggests a powerful way of making prayer more personal, more emotional, and more physical. We often speak of "enlightenment" and "illumination," but these words are in danger of becoming empty symbols. The meaning becomes much clearer when we light candles in the dark sanctuary while singing, "Shine on me, shine on me; let the light from the lighthouse shine on me," or "Silently now I wait for thee, ready, my God, thy will to see; Open my eyes, illumine me, Spirit divine."

Because reading poses such a problem, we do not want to have many written prayers in worship services that include those who happen to be mentally challenged. If you do use written prayers, give the worshipers a part that they can repeat. Remember before the praying starts to share that part with the worshipers and have them practice it before prayer begins.

Relying on printed materials is a not very subtle way of separating those who can read from those who can't. Many persons who happen to be mentally challenged do not accept this distinction. Clara is not the only one in our congregation who likes to hold reading materials when everyone else is doing so. Sometimes the book is right-side-up. At other times it is upside-down. Because reading isn't the issue in our congregation, it doesn't matter how Clara holds her book. The distinctions of ability between Clara and other worshipers disappear.

If the Lord's Prayer is part of your regular worship, make sure everyone knows the words. Try singing the prayer and *signing* the prayer at least some of the time. Many of those who happen to be mentally challenged have learned American Sign Language in order to compensate for limited speaking ability.

If you think of prayer as direct immediate communication with God, the presence of persons who happen to be mentally challenged will present no hindrance whatsoever. Indeed, that presence will be a benefit and blessing for all who pray.

Although we believe that a significant amount of silence is a good idea in all Christian worship, silence is especially appropriate when the congregation is diverse. First, if prayer is two-way communication, there must be some listening in it. Also, you may well be surprised by the utterances that find their way into the silence that you have created.

Gertrude expressed her need for inward silence at one Christmas morning Communion service when she was asked to pray. She closed her eyes and drew a very deep breath. There was a long, long pause. Finally she spoke. "Thank You, Jesus, for being born at Christmas and for giving us this bread. We love You very, very much. Amen." Those who were present believe that nowhere in all Christendom was a more elegant and eloquent prayer of blessing offered up that Christmas morning.

Nevertheless, a word of caution is needed now. It is no accident that traditional worship is full of noise. Silence can be threatening. It makes us vulnerable. It is in understanding such simple things that we can anticipate persons' opposition. We can therefore decide beforehand and on purpose how we are going to deal with their reluctance to undergo change.

Confession is especially powerful prayer when those who happen to be mentally challenged are included. Remind the congregation that all sin causes at least three kinds of damage: damage to God, damage to self, and damage to others. Confession should address all three dimensions. Many persons who happen to be mentally challenged will surprise you with how freely they are willing to offer their confession to other actual human beings.

We can easily accentuate the physical power of prayer by paying attention to body posture. During Lent, we can pass out pretzel twists to taste, hold, look at and then imitate by praying with crossed arms. Isaiah 1:1, 10-20 suggests spreading our hands out in prayer (verse 15) so we could hold our arms outstretched and sing one stanza of "It's me, it's me, it's me, O Lord, standing in the need of prayer."

Isaiah 1:16 suggests another possibility. The verse says, "Wash and make yourself clean," so literally washing with soap and water helps us understand how we might "wash away" an undesirable behavior.

These examples show how our prayer life can be greatly enriched and emotionally expanded. We take the symbolic meaning back to its basis in physical experience and are reminded, perhaps, of the kind of praying that happens when we are kneeling by our bedsides or praying in a circle of persons holding each other's hands.

Scripture

Because we Christians are known as "People of the Book," it may seem difficult to include serious interaction with the Bible in a worship experience that tries specifically to include those who happen to be mentally challenged. Many of the apparent difficulties can be avoided by applying the principles of **"P-E-P."**

One **"P-E-P"** principle is to not require reading. Whatever can be read can also be read *aloud*. Furthermore, the text can be read aloud in more than one way. We needn't confine the reading to either one person or one time. After all, the more often we hear something (and in a greater variety of ways), the more likely we are to understand and remember what we have heard. For example, we might present Philippians 2:5-11 not only as a reading but also by singing one of the hymn versions of the passage, such as "At the

Name of Jesus" or "All Hail the Power of Jesus' Name."

Even so, there is one apparently unavoidable hurdle when it comes to interacting with the Bible. One cannot do "serious Bible study" if that phrase means "identifying and reflecting upon the abstract meanings of the passage." Of course, that's not all that "serious Bible study" means. We can study the text through the experience of it. When a specific text is presented personally, emotionally and physically, we are doing *experiential* Bible study.

Role-play, drama, image journeys, puppetry, flannelgraph, and object lessons are some of the strategies we might use. There are also dance and drawing. To discover how to use these techniques in actual worship events, see the examples in Part Two.

Another way of making the "reading" of Scripture more accessible to all is especially worthy of mention. We can tell rather than read the passage. This choice requires more careful preparation, but the increased impact makes it well worth the additional time and energy expended.

We memorize the text directly from the Scripture and then speak it in a relaxed and natural way as though it were our own words. There is a captivating quality in telling and hearing the Scripture in this fashion. Both speaker and listener are available for connection. The storyteller's energy is directed outward to the listeners rather than downward to the book. The listeners are in communication with the teller because they are seeing each other, not merely listening.

The Sermon

We first began to suspect there was an important learning about the preaching event when we noticed that more people sat up and took notice at the children's sermon than at the adult sermon. People smiled and nodded. They were really listening. They were sitting on the edges of their seats and paying full attention. During the adult sermon, many sat back in the pew—passive listeners.

In most congregations biblical interpretation occurs during the sermon. If you have a sermon in your church but still want to include those who happen to be mentally challenged, the main thing to be sure of is that the language of the sermon is not propositional (that is, ideas that call for intellectual response).

Instead, the sermon might take the form of a story. Many churches, of course, are already doing this. The power of story is being reclaimed. This is the kind of language that shows up in the Bible. *The United Methodist Book of Worship* offers an excellent example of how Scripture stories can be used effectively to replace the sermon. "The Passion Story may be read dramatically, with members of the congregation taking the various roles" (*The United Methodist Book of Worship*: Nashville, TN; p. 340). We offer another version of the Passion Story in the worship material contained in Part Two of this book.

For those congregations willing to take an even bigger chance, we suggest no traditional sermon at all. Instead, when it comes time to respond to the Scripture, divide the congregation into small groups. Assign them the task of developing the proclamation themselves. In this process they will be unpacking the meanings of Scripture for themselves and applying those meanings to the specific situations of their lives.

The possibilities of this more radical alternative are almost endless. Just remember to follow these few simple guidelines:

◆ Each small group should be representative of the entire congregation, but if you want most people to do some abstract reflecting, this guideline can be waived. In this case, you will need to design a separate activity for those persons who happen to be mentally challenged.

◆ Each group should have at least one leader who is sensitive to the strengths and limitations of persons who happen to be mentally challenged.

◆ Point the groups' discussion by using questions that persons can respond to in personal and emotional terms.

Forming groups to wrestle with the meanings of Joshua 3:7-17, the group leaders might ask questions like these: Did you ever step into a fast-running river? What was the experience like? What did you see, hear, and feel as the water rushed around your feet? Such questions are examples of making the passage more personal and physical. These questions give the worshipers a non-abstract point of entry into the text.

Continue the discussion with similar questions. How do you feel when you have to try something you have never done before? This question personalizes and emotionalizes verses 14-16. The physical meaning is that the priests were stepping into water. The more abstract meaning is that they were "stepping out in faith."

Or ask, "If you had been one of the people that day at the Jordan River, what might you have said when you saw 'the water pile up in one place'?" This question invites the people to identify themselves among God's people then and now.

A final question might be, "What miracles of God's working in the world have you seen?" So we personalize by connecting the Scripture account to these persons' lives.

You will see in the orders of worship that follow many examples of forms of proclamation—visuals, music, drama, movement and dance—that do not rely upon intellectual abstraction.

Response to the Word

To most worship designers, "response to the Word" is a catch phrase. They mean by it the offering, Communion, and altar call. But "response to the Word" is really a very big idea. It includes the offering of concerns, prayers, gifts and service to the world and one another. None of these pieces of worship presents any special problem when the congregation includes persons who happen to be mentally challenged.

By early in the third century, the Church had resolved the *pistis-gnosis* conflict. *Pistis* is the Greek word for "faith." *Gnosis* is Greek for "knowledge." Gnostics were people who said that faithfulness was a matter of possessing secret knowledge that led to salvation. Orthodox Christianity decided long ago that faith is not primarily a matter of intellectual understanding.

So *pistis* was declared the winner. Faith won out over knowledge. The victory means that people who happen to be mentally challenged can still say yes to an altar call, still offer their time, money and promises to do specific ministries, and still decide for themselves whether and how to participate in the Lord's Supper.

Response to the Word for persons who happen to be mentally challenged works out like this. The worship leaders must become acquainted with the gifts and abilities of each worshiper (personalizing). When the worshipers are singled out for individual recognition, they experience being known and valued. There is an increase of self-esteem (emotionalizing). Acts of ministry, discipleship and service appropriate to each person are suggested to the worshipers (physicalizing).

For example, eight-year-old Devante folds the bulletins. Ten-year-old Rolf shovels the sidewalk east of the building. Curtis, who happens to be mentally challenged, passes out the bulletins. Audrey, who also happens to be mentally challenged, shakes hands with entering worshipers. Can we find a way to use Betty's enjoyment of making bead necklaces? Perhaps we could use beadwork on Bible bookmarks to give to shut-ins during Lent.

The Lord's Supper

Congregations with specific requirements for participation in Communion can tell those requirements before the Meal and then be sure that those requirements are met. In our congregation, we offer with the Supper additional alternatives like pieces of fresh fruit and miniature whole-grain muffins. The message is that all present are children of God whether or not they have identified themselves as Christian disciples. All have a place in the worshipping community by virtue of the simple facts of their humanity and presence. The Bread and Cup are reserved for those who have declared themselves to be Christian disciples.

A Glimpse of the Bigger Picture

Discovering and naming the strengths of those who happen to be mentally challenged raises a host of questions. What if Gospel living requires including not only those who happen to be mentally challenged but also all sorts of other folks who manifest a wide variety of other kinds of difference? For example, and it is only an example, in our congregation there are a number of Hispanic persons for whom English is very much a second language. Most Christians would agree, perhaps after a bit of reflection, that we are not being fair to our Hispanic sisters and brothers when we conduct the entire life of the congregation in English.

The simple admission of justice, however, does not go deep enough. The deeper truth is that we Anglos will ourselves be greatly blessed if and when we start to learn

Spanish. Imitating the love of God in Christ Jesus is a wonderfully surprising adventure. Instead of drawing lines of protection that separate us from others, we discover that their very difference is a blessing for us. We open ourselves to those differences, and they change us. They make us grow, which means becoming more whole.

Alas, there are hidden subtle pitfalls along the way that can make us stumble and show up our secret attitudes of exclusivity. For example, what is the message delivered when we serve the children and those who happen to be mentally challenged at the church potluck, if everyone else goes through the line and serves themselves? The answer is that rather than promoting wholeness and power, we are encouraging them to be dependent and weak.

It is tempting to settle for the easier way, rather than to deal with balance and coordination problems that may require a personal escort from buffet line to table. If efficiency wins out, it is a Pyrrhic victory. The values of autonomy, self-reliance and the preciousness of each human spirit have been swept aside.

The potluck question is resolved only to be replaced by another manifestation of itself in new guise. For example, one Sunday during the coffee fellowship Dorothy broke a cup. It was not a big deal. It was something that could happen to anyone, except Dorothy happens to be mentally challenged. Immediately, Dorothy and the other residents of the Jackson Center were told to sit down. Women of the congregation began to deliver cups of coffee to them.

The significance was not lost on Dorothy. The blow

to her self-esteem was sharp. Dorothy felt obliged to apolo-
gize at least three times for breaking the cup. She tried to
explain over and over again to one of the pastors, "I didn't
mean to do it. I'm sorry."

Being truly welcoming means treating everyone the
same. The same standards are applied across the board—to
women and men alike, to laity and clergy, to those with
different abilities; indeed, to everyone present. Would the
pastor have been pointedly told to sit down and wait to have
a cup of coffee delivered, had it been the pastor who had
broken a cup?

Accidents are accidents. They can happen to anyone.
The consequences of actions must be the same for all. What
is the worth of a coffee cup compared to the worth of
Dorothy's spirit? The Christian folk hymn says, "They will
know we are Christians when we guard each one's dignity and
save each one's pride," not when we have the highest number
possible of unbroken coffee cups at the end of the year.

Working to fit worship to the strengths and limitations of everyone isn't easy. There are so many hidden
assumptions that can rear their ugly heads and unexpectedly
take control. But the quality of the trophy makes it worth
running the race, and outrunning our ingrained prejudices.

Those who happen to be mentally challenged, persons
of different ethnicity, children, the poor (and the very rich of
course!)—where does it end? Addressing persons where they
are is simply another name for Gospel living. If Jesus is right,
the yoke is easy, the burden is light, and one of the major
fruits is joy.

What About the Rest of the Congregation?

So far we've been lifting up the joy and delight of Gospel living, but there is also a shadow side to Christian discipleship. Make no mistake, no congregation can radically re-conceptualize its worship life without experiencing all sorts of additional, unanticipated changes. If you plan and implement worship that is significantly different from how it has always been, you will inevitably experience even more differences within your congregation than you initially bargained for. Some of those differences are likely to become quite unpleasant indeed.

For congregations which decide to be more inclusive, we make three predictions. First, there will be a contingent in your congregation that strongly resists innovation. Some of these folks may stop coming to your church, unless and until you return to traditional ways. Second, there will be members, notably adolescents, who will be reluctant to participate fully in the new worship style. Their resistance, however, will not be so strong that it drives them away. Third, the changes you make will be wonderfully enlivening for some members, especially (but not exclusively) the children. Your new worship style will result in a significant increase of first-time worship attenders.

The challenge is to respond appropriately when all three of these predictions come true. They will only happen after you have made substantial changes in the way you worship. In fact, many churches will decide they have experienced enough change before that time arrives. For these churches, we modify our third prediction to say, a core group will form in your church. They will be energized by the changes and eager to share their new energy, both inside and outside the congregation.

If you change greatly, however, you will need to be sensitive and responsive to the results in your congregational life. For example, you will need to be very patient with the first group, those who are very distressed by the changes. You must both go slowly and explain what you are doing and why you are doing it. These people need to understand the changes that are happening, and they need substantial advance notice.

You may decide that they have the right to preserve those portions of the worship service that they value most highly. For example, if you decide to divide into small groups for the Gospel proclamation as an alternative to the traditional sermon, you may include a mini-sermon for these persons. It will probably be important to them to have the pastor deliver it. At bare minimum, you must not try to coerce them into accepting newness. Coercion is seldom effective in actually producing change, and it clearly does not fit with the Gospel message you are trying to live.

In fact, since this first group is likely to be the hard core, you may not have too many real choices. We believe that some of the choices are more righteous than others.

The worst choice, we think, would be to accept these folks' using the change as a catalyst for an all-out power struggle and then to either give up or fight. Giving up means returning to the old ways, leaving those who happen to be mentally challenged at the fringe of the congregation. Fighting is admitting defeat. By fighting you succumb to the sinful urge to draw lines of separation and build walls of exclusion—the very thing that you have been working to avoid.

You may be part of a very remarkable congregation in which the first prediction never does come true, but if opposition should arise, think about regarding the unpleasantness as an invitation. Do you have two worship spaces in your building? If so, consider letting fierce opponents have a worship service of their own. Of course, if they are the majority or you have another good reason, you may decide simply to withdraw the innovations to another setting and let the majority return to the status quo.

The second possibility is to divide the worshipers into different time slots. One thing we know about groups is that they, like individuals, have life cycles. Groups are born, develop and die. We know that groups are at their most vitally attractive when they are relatively new. What appears to be a split, division and loss can actually become a means of congregational growth. Even the "traditionalists" might grow if they find themselves in a new space, at a new time, and with some new persons in their midst.

Of course, there is a worst case scenario. If the highly resistant group is very small, you may simply prefer —reluctantly—to let them go. After all, there are many churches with worship formats designed to make them feel right at home.

The counsel with regard to those who are reluctant but not in danger of leaving is also patience and respect. It is no accident that congregations tend to be relatively homogeneous. It is hard for everyone to incorporate other styles and viewpoints. Especially in adolescence it is terribly difficult to be different. Some of us will outgrow that stage if we are dealt with patiently. Even those of us who never do outgrow our resistance may find, over time, that our resistance is less.

The third prediction, that there will be new life, is the happiest one. All sorts of exciting experiments might be run in a congregation that is on the cutting edge of change. Even if this group is at first much smaller, it is the one that bears the most growth potential.

You can expect that this third group will constitute a warm welcoming cadre for persons who happen to be mentally challenged. Their presence will be leaven in the larger congregation. With appropriate management skills you can continue living with these tensions for a very long time.

Leaven, you will remember, works quietly while hidden inside. It sometimes takes leaven a long time to accomplish its purpose, but, nevertheless, leaven is a very good image for the Kingdom of God.

Part Two:
Practical Applications

All of these worship activities were created for use in a congregation that attempts to practice full inclusivity. A congregation just beginning to worship in new ways will probably not be ready for all these suggestions. We propose two modifications. First, you could change only one or two "pieces" of worship. Or you could make many small changes in the entire service.

Churches that have pews bolted to the floor will need to examine all of the suggestions that have to do with movement. Make the adjustments that fit your physical space. There are also limitations of emotion and attitude. Count the cost of this tower you are planning to build. Make an intelligent and realistic assessment of your congregation's willingness to change.

For example, a time of genuine greeting is easier to accept than new ways of delivering a sermon. Conduct a survey of your congregation. Discover what they value most in worship now. Then select what works for you from the following examples.

Finally, remember there is nothing magic about our examples. You will find some things useful and others not. You will also make some new discoveries of your own. We would very much appreciate your letting us know what you learn. Write us at Broken Walls Christian Community, 617 W. Washington Street, Milwaukee, WI 53204.

In the following orders of worship, we use brackets for explanation. The words inside brackets would not appear in the actual worship bulletins.

The First Worship Service: "Kindred in Christ"

Greeting and Welcome

[*Second Corinthians 8:7 is the basis for this part of worship. The passage reads, "See that you also excel in this grace of giving."*

[*Play the music that will be used in worship as the people arrive. Invite persons to assist with various tasks in order to prepare for worship.*

[*Some of these jobs might be to . . .*

- *fold bulletins*
- *arrange seating*
- *greet arriving worshipers*
- *distribute bulletins*
- *distribute name tags and markers*
- *create decoration for the worship space*
- *prepare the Scripture reading from Mark 5:21-43*
- *learn "the action chant" and/or prepare special music]*

Call to Worship (from Second Corinthians 8:9, responsively)

[*As always when some of the congregation can't read, teach the congregation its part, and practice until they have mastered it.*]

All: We know the grace of our Lord Jesus Christ.

Leader I: That though he was rich, yet for our sakes he became poor.

46

All: We know the grace of our Lord Jesus Christ.

Leader II: So that we through his poverty might become rich.

All: We know the grace of our Lord Jesus Christ.

Hymn: "Rejoice, the Lord Is King"

[Remember the non-readers. Teach the repeated line, "Lift up your heart, life up your voice! Rejoice; again I say rejoice!"]

Opening Prayer and Praise

[The worship leader reads Genesis 4:3-10. After the reading divide into groups of four to six persons.

[Everybody makes their body into a statue of Cain. All the "statues" report how they feel. They try to imagine how Cain himself might have been feeling. Then they make themselves into statues of Abel and report what they are feeling and how Abel might have felt.

[Invite groups to discuss how it feels to treat each other as sisters and brothers. Remind them that, unlike Cain, we know that we are supposed to take care of each other.

[Ask each small group to choose an action they will do that shows taking care of our sisters and brothers in Christ. Some responses might be to give and get hugs, say "God bless you," and pat someone on the back.

[The groups share their answers with each other and then close this activity by praying together.]

Response by the People: "We Are One in the Bond of Love" (or "We Are the Church")

[Form two circles, one inside the other (either two large circles or, depending upon the setup of the sanctuary, a number of smaller circles). While singing the first verse, the inner circle moves clockwise, and the outer circle moves counterclockwise. Each person waves, smiles, shakes hands or bows a greeting to members of the other circle as they pass each other.

[On the second verse, both circles turn in to face the center. Members of the inner circle, still holding hands, raise their arms to form a series of arches. Members of the outer circle, still holding hands, come under the arches, and the members of the inner circle drop their arms. All are now linked in a bond of love.

[Stand and sway while singing the first verse again. It is helpful to have musicians doing "back-up" while the congregation dances. Then you might trade jobs, offering to sing for the musicians so they can dance too. Some people will never feel free to dance unless and until they receive encouragement.]

Scripture Lesson: Second Corinthians 8:7-15

Special Music

Gospel Lesson: Mark 5:21-43

[Readers of the Gospel and leaders of the action chant rehearsed during the time of worship preparation.

Reader I (male): Vss. 21-24
Reader II (female): Vss. 25-29
Reader I: Vss. 30-32
Reader II: Vss. 33-34
Reader I: Vs. 35
Reader II: Vss. 36-39
Reader I: Vss. 40-41
Reader II: Vss. 42-43]

Action Chant

[Begin with everyone sitting. Always, when using movement in worship, remember that some persons have limited mobility. Give everyone permission to restrict their movements to whatever extent they must.

[Invite the congregation to imitate the gestures of the leaders.]

Little girl was lying in her bed.
> *[All lay their heads on hands to indicate sleeping.]*

Everybody thought that she was dead.
> *[Cross arms over chest, hands touching shoulders.]*

They had all been crying; their eyes were red.
> *[Twists fists at corners of eyes.]*

Along came Jesus, and he said,
> *[Use hands to sign "walking."]*

"Little girl, arise!"
> *[Turn palms up; raise hands toward ceiling.]*

She opened her eyes.

> *[Hold fists at eye level, and pop fists open
> to emphasize the image of popeyed surprise.]*

What a surprise!

> *[Clap hands.]*

She jumped out of bed.

> *[All stand quickly. Remember, some persons
> are not able to stand.]*

Then Jesus said, "She needs to be fed."

> *[Mime holding soup bowl and eating with
> spoon. Repeat the action chant at least once
> so everyone is able to participate.]*

Sermon   *[There is no traditional sermon. Instead, the
entire service interprets and proclaims the
scriptural meanings.]*

Response to the Word: "There Is a Balm in Gilead"
*[Remember that "call-and-response" allows everyone
to participate.]*

Offering

Leader: ". . . If the willingness is there, the gift is
acceptable according to what one has, not
according to what one does not have."

(Second Corinthians 8:12)

*[Discuss in pairs what each person has done in this
service. What new thing might you do to treat persons as
sisters and brothers this week? Allow enough time to share.]*

Thanksgiving: "Praise God from Whom All Blessings Flow"

The Lord's Prayer

Benediction

[Each person should choose a single behavior that shows kindred care. Everyone shares their choices. For example, shake hands and say, "God bless you."]

The Second Worship Service: FaithWalk

Greeting and Welcome
[Help everyone prepare for worship with the musical offering, "Precious Lord, Take My Hand."]

Call to Worship: Psalm 5:8; "Lead Me, Lord"

Lead me, Lord. Lead me in Your righteousness.
Make Your way plain before my face.

[This Scripture ties in with Hebrews 11:3. Ask worshipers to line up single file with their hands on the shoulders of the person in front of them. All close their eyes. The leader guides them in a snake dance through the sanctuary while all sing. The movement should be slow, smooth and rhythmic.]

Opening Prayer and Praise
[Everyone forms a prayer circle around the altar or worship center. Before sitting, persons may report their experiences of walking without sight.]

Hymn: "Open My Eyes, That I May See"

[The refrain invites participation by all. Teach the refrain before singing.]

Prayer of Confession

52

[Ask worshipers to tell what people can do with their eyes closed (for example, think, listen to music, pray, sleep). Now ask what happens when our eyes are closed when they should be open (for example, we miss important things; people trip and fall down). Say, "That's what Jesus is talking about in this passage," *and then read Luke 12:35-40.*

[Now the leader says, "We are God's servants. We need to be awake and alert. But first, let's close our eyes."

[The leader holds up a large picture of a current world problem and says, "In a moment I'm going to have you open your eyes. Sometimes we don't want to see what is going on around us. But Jesus says we need to pay attention. So now open your eyes, and if you have something to pray about this picture, go ahead and pray it aloud."

[The leader echoes some of the prayers and then adds, "Open my eyes; illumine me, Spirit Divine." *Continue this process with other pictures. Be sure to include pictures that depict various levels of human activity. For example, show pictures of homeless persons, senior citizens, hungry children and environmental damage.*

[Conclude confession by saying something like, "Help us, O God, to stay awake and alert to do Your will in the world." *Then sing again "Lead Me, Lord."]*

Words of Assurance: Hebrews 11:1-3

Response by the People: "Soon and Very Soon"
[Invite worshipers to cover their eyes until the last line, "Hallelujah! Hallelujah! We're going to see the King."]

Old Testament Lesson: Second Kings 17:33-40

Special Music: "We Walk by Faith and Not By Sight"

Epistle Lesson: Hebrews 11:1-3, 8-12

Hymn: "He Leadeth Me, O Blessed Thought"
[Accentuate the repeated refrain to encourage everyone to sing.]

Sermon
[This form of sermon is in experience rather than mere words. The experience is based on the Scripture lessons. In pairs, have one person lead another, blindfolded, throughout the worship space. Designate stations to which all are lead. Include such activities as these.

- ◆ *touch the water in the baptismal font or hear the splash of water in the baptistry*
- ◆ *feel a stained-glass window*
- ◆ *smell a flower*
- ◆ *feel a flower's petals on one's cheek*
- ◆ *hear a door creak, or push open a door and feel and smell the new air*
- ◆ *touch velvet draperies or cushions, or the roughness of exposed brick*
- ◆ *listen to piano strings strummed by hand*
- ◆ *taste grape juice*
- ◆ *listen by earphones to a soloist sing, "Precious Lord, Take My Hand"*

◆ *At some point, a surprise for everyone.
(See Luke 12:40. Make sure the
surprise is pleasant, not startling.)]*

Offering

Leader: The Lord, who brought you up out of Egypt
with mighty power and outstretched arm, is the one you must
worship. To Him you shall bow down and to Him offer
sacrifices.   (Second Kings 17:36)

Doxology

Prayer of Thanksgiving

The Lord's Prayer

Benediction

*[Invite all to share their discoveries about "walking by
faith" or "living alert to do God's will." Include some of
these sharings in the prayer of benediction. The final action
is everyone's turning toward the main exit to represent
returning to the world and singing "Lead Me, Lord."]*

The Third Worship Service: Get on the Right Path

[This service assumes that you have a long, narrow sanctuary with a single aisle. If not, you will have to make some modifications.]

Coming Together

[In the narthex make a fold-over name tag for each worshiper. Make the outside of the tag look like a gift box. Inside, draw or cut and paste from a magazine a picture that represents this person's special gift from God. For example, Betty has a picture of beads because she likes to string bead necklaces. Pearl has a smiling face because she is always warm and welcoming. Audrey's tag has a picture of hands because, although she cannot talk, she always shakes hands.

[Matthew 23:12 ("Whoever exalts himself will be humbled, and whoever humbles himself will be exalted") is the basis of this activity. We are both proud and humble because of these characteristics—proud because they are gifts from God; humble for just the same reason.]

Call to Worship

[In the narthex, a soloist sings the first two stanzas of "O for a Heart to Praise My God."]

Invocation

Confession

[*Gather the congregation at the back of the sanctuary. Prepare enough poster boards with large red circles to fill your space.*

[*Two readers present Malachi 2:5-10—the first reader doing vss. 5-7, the second reader doing vss. 8-10. Ask how people "turn from the way" (vs. 8). Write each answer in a circle on the poster board. Take a strip of red sticky tape to make a slash through the circle to represent a traffic sign's "No!" Pair a reader and non-reader to hold and interpret each sign. Station the pairs in various places in the sanctuary so they block access to the chancel.*

[*Before the journey begins, a soloist sings the first and third stanzas of "O for a Heart to Praise My God." Musicians can provide "traveling music" during the journey. Possible songs include "O Master, Let Me Walk with Thee," "Camina, Pueblo de Dios," "I Want to Walk as a Child of the Light." or "Guide Me, O Thou Great Jehovah."*

[*Don't neglect worshipers of limited mobility. For example, you might need a special wheelchair route that can also be used by persons who have difficulty walking.*

[*Tell everyone they are to try to reach the chancel. The worshipers must go through the maze. Whenever the travelers encounter a pair with a sign, the reader reads the sign, and both say together, "You've turned from the way." The traveler must then try to find another route.*

[*Seat the congregation in the front pews. Line up the sign-holding pairs. The soloist sings stanzas one and four of "O for a Heart to Praise My God." Each pair explains their sign.   Each explanation ends with the congregation's response:]*

People: We have turned from the way.

Words of Assurance (from First Thessalonians 2:13)

> Leader: The Word of God is at work in you who believe.

Response of the People
[The soloist leads the congregation in the first stanza of "O for a Heart to Praise My God." Since the worshipers have heard the stanza three times, they will be able to sing along.]

Epistle Lesson: First Thessalonians 2:7-13

Hymn: "Guide Me, O Thou Great Jehovah"

Gospel Lesson: Matthew 23:1-12

Proclamation: "Get on the Right Path"
[Small groups take the place of a traditional sermon. Leaders ask questions like these: Have you ever gotten lost? How did you feel? How did you get found? What happens when we get lost from God's path, and how do we feel? How do we get back on the right path, and how do we feel then?]

Offering

[The worship leader may say, "God gives gifts to each one of us so that we can share in God's work in the world. What is your gift? How will you use it?"

[Everyone turns to a neighbor and shares their name tag gift and their intention for using it.]

Thanksgiving

[Everyone should process solemnly to the Lord's Table. If Communion is celebrated, the nearness will help worshipers participate fully. Conclude the thanksgiving with words like these: "God gave us the greatest gift of all, God's Own Self." *Then everyone prays the Lord's Prayer.]*

Hymn: "O for a Heart to Praise My God" *(first stanza)*

Shared Blessing (from First Thessalonians 2:13)

[Teach these words to the congregation so each person can share the blessing with others. The blessing is, "The Word of God . . . is at work in you who believe."*]*

The Fourth Worship Service: "Hosanna!"

Greeting and Welcome
>*[Play spirited marching music as worshipers gather. Possible choices include "Lead on, O King Eternal," "Come We Who Love the Lord" and "Onward Christian Soldiers." Worshipers help each other make pompons from rolled newspapers.]*

Call to Worship (from Isaiah 59:20-21, responsively)
>*[Explain that "hosanna" means "God saves" and was a Hebrew shout or cheer.]*

Leader I:	God says to the people,
Leader II:	The Redeemer will come to *[name of your community]*, to those in Jacob who repent of their sins.
People:	**Hosanna!**
Leader I:	This is my covenant with them, says the Lord. My Spirit, who is on you, and my words that I have put in your mouth will not depart from your mouth,
People:	**Hosanna!**
Leader II:	Or from the mouths of your children, or from the mouths of their descendants from this time on and forever.
People:	**Hosanna!**

Hymn: "Hail to the Lord's Anointed"
[Invite everyone to parade through the worship space. At the end of each stanza allow time for all to shout "Hosanna!"and shake their pompons.]

Call to Confession: First Timothy 1:12-16
[After a brief silence to reflect on the reading, invite the congregation to move about the worship space. When persons encounter others they have hurt or offended, they should ask for forgiveness.]

Words of Assurance (from Luke 23:34)

Leader: Jesus said, "Father, forgive them."

Response of the People: First Timothy 1:17
[This is an echo chant. Worshipers repeat each phrase after the leader.]

> Now to the King eternal . . .
> Immortal, invisible . . .
> The only God . . .
> Be honor and glory . . .
> For ever and ever . . .
> Amen.

Hymn: "Immortal, Invisible, God Only Wise"

Old Testament Lesson: Isaiah 59:14-20

Psalm (from 118:1-4, 19, 26, responsively)
[Teach the response, "God's love endures forever," sung to the first seven notes of "Lead on, O King Eternal."]

Leader: Give thanks to the Lord for he is good. His love endures forever. Let Israel say:

People *(sung):* **God's love endures forever.**

Leader: Let the house of Aaron say:

People *(sung)*: **God's love endures forever.**

Leader: Let those who fear the Lord say:

People *(sung)*: **God's love endures forever.**

Leader: Open for me the gates of righteousness. I will enter and give thanks to the Lord.

People *(sung)*: **God's love endures forever.**

Leader: Blessed is he who comes in the name of the Lord. From the house of the Lord we bless you.

People *(sung)*: **God's love endures forever.**

Gospel Lesson: Luke 19:28-40

Action Chant
[This chant is even more fun with choreographed movement and pompons.]
When Jesus came to town . . . *[march in place]*
The people gathered round . . . *[left hand on hip, right hand outstretched; bounce pompon in rhythm]*

They shouted . . . *[both hands on hips]*
Hosanna! *[raise pompon over head; then lower]*
Hosanna! *[repeat action with pompon]*
Praise be to God! *[shake pompon vigorously]*
Blessed is he . . . *[make figure-eight with pompon]*
Who comes in the name of the Lord
　　　　　[repeat figure-eight]
Hosanna! *[raise pompon over head]*

Prayer

[Depending on size of the congregation, either pass a large (three to five pounds is about right) stone, or distribute palm-size stones to everyone. Say, "Listen to the stone. This was one of the stones in the road when Jesus came by."

[Wait. Allow time for people to listen with "the ears of their ears." Then invite everyone to share what they have "heard."]

Song: "When Jesus Wept"

[Explain that the Palm Sunday celebration is incomplete without recognition of the coming Passion. Teach the song.   Then sing as a "layered song."   Divide congregation into four groups. The first group sings "When Jesus wept, the falling tear" eight times. After the first singing, the second group enters with "in mercy flowed beyond all bound," which they sing six times. When the second group starts its first repetition, the third group enters with "when Jesus groaned, a trembling fear," which they sing four times.

When the third group starts its first repetition, the fourth group enters with "seized all the guilty world around," which they sing twice.]

Sermon

> *[Use a story or dramatic reading of the Passion. See, for example, the script at the end of this book.]*

Offering

Prayer of Thanksgiving

The Lord's Prayer

Song: "Jesus, Remember Me"

Benediction: Luke 19:38, responsively

Leader:	Blessed is the king who comes in the name of the Lord!
People:	**Hosanna!**
Leader:	Peace in heaven and glory in the highest!
People:	**Hosanna!**

The Fifth Worship Service: "Emmaus Eyes"

Greeting and Welcome

[Teach the congregation the music to be used in this service. The tambourine players practice their part for the "Moses and Miriam Chant."]

Call to Worship

Leader:	Christ is risen!
People:	**Christ is risen!**
Leader:	He is risen indeed.
People:	**He is risen indeed!**
Leader:	Alleluia!
People:	**Alleluia!**

Hymn: "Christ the Lord Is Risen Today"

Invocation: "Moses and Miriam Chant"

[Use tambourines to keep the beat. Do a shake on the words "gloriously" and "sea." Repeat the chant several times. Moses and Miriam may exchange lines.]

Moses *(all men)*:	God has triumphed gloriously.
Miriam *(all women)*:	Horse and rider are thrown in the sea.

Choral Reading: First Corinthians 15:20-26

[Use the church choir or form a special speaking choir.]

Reader I: Christ has indeed been raised from the dead.

Chorus: The first fruits . . .

Men: Of those who have fallen asleep.

Women: Who have fallen asleep.

Reader II: For since death came through a man . . .

Reader I: The resurrection of the dead comes also through a man.

Chorus: For as in Adam all die . . .

Men: So in Christ, all will be made alive.

Reader II: But each in his own turn:

Chorus: Christ, the first fruits.

Women: Then when he comes, those who belong to him.

Reader I: Then the end will come

Reader II: When he hands over the kingdom
to God the Father.

Reader I: After he has destroyed all dominion,

Men: Authority

Women: And power.

Men: For he must reign . . .

Women: Until he has put all of his enemies under his feet.

Reader II: The last enemy to be destroyed is . . .

Chorus: Death.

Hymn: "Thine Be the Glory"
[The repeated words of the refrain permit a greater degree of participation.]

Old Testament Lesson: Exodus 15:1-11

Gospel Lesson: Luke 24:13-35

Sermon

[Show the congregation a variety of artists' conceptions of Jesus. Be sure to include work of Native Americans, African Americans and Hispanics as well as those from other ethnic groups. Encourage worshipers to share which images seem most engaging to them.]

Confession

[Teach the congregation its part, and allow them to practice before actually doing the litany. As always, feel free to modify the service to fit your needs. Here, for example, there may be specific petitions you need to make because of the special characteristics of your situation.]

Leader:	Lord Jesus, you are walking among us every day in the streets of our city . . .
People:	**Forgive us when we do not recognize you.**
Leader:	You are the hungry and the homeless . . .
People:	**Forgive us when we do not recognize you.**

Leader:	You are the sick and the lonely . . .
People:	**Forgive us when we do not recognize you.**
Leader:	You are among the victims of violence and with the neglected and abused . . .
People:	**Forgive us when we do not recognize you.**
Leader:	You, O Lord, greet us with your peace.
People:	**Forgive us when we do not recognize you.**

Words of Assurance (from Luke 24:30-31)

[Station worship leaders throughout the space so each leader can be seen by only a portion of the congregation.

[Use a variety of different breads—tortilla, corn bread, Indian fry bread, rice cakes, pumpernickel. Break the breads and have persons describe what they see. Encourage persons to see that the varieties of bread are similar to the varieties of images of Jesus. Conclude with the words . . .]

Leader:	Their eyes were opened, and they recognized him.

Response of the People: "Morning Has Broken"

Offering

Thanksgiving

68

[Celebrate an Agape Meal. Use the breads that were previously broken plus milk and honey. Early Christians drank milk and honey as a reminder of the Promised Land. This old-fashioned baby formula is especially appropriate for the day that celebrates the new birth of all creation.]

Benediction

[Hold an accordion folded piece of paper so it is only a single strip wide. Bend paper at its midpoint and imitate a caterpillar inching its way along. Remind everyone how the caterpillar wraps itself in a cocoon and seems dead, only to suddenly burst forth as a butterfly. Open the paper bow-tie fashion, pinching the middle. The result will look like a butterfly, which is a traditional symbol for the Resurrection. Ask if anyone can tell why.

[Make butterflies by randomly coloring both sides of sheets of paper. Accordion fold the paper, pinch it in the middle like a bow tie, and secure it by gluing two cigar-shaped pieces of paper together. Suspend the butterflies on string throughout the worship space, or let the people take them home as souvenirs of worship.]

Song: "Praise Ye the Lord" (or Hymn: "Christ Rose")

Shared Blessing

Leader: Christ is risen!
People: **Christ is risen!**
Leader: He is risen indeed.

People: **He is risen indeed!**
Leader: Alleluia!
People: **Alleluia!**

A Passion Play: "At the Place Called The Skull"
~ Luke 23:1-49 ~

Production Notes

This dramatic treatment has been prepared especially for persons who happen to be mentally challenged. We intend it as an expression of interdependence of all members of the Body of Christ. It yokes a reader and non-reader in a common task. Two persons are required for each speaking role, the Character and the Character's Shadow. The Character is dependent upon the Shadow for a voice, and the Shadow relies upon the Character for a body. Characters perform the dramatic action in mime. They are coached, *sotto voce*, by their Shadows.

The Shadows carry copies of the script and read the narrative portions, addressing the audience. Lines of Character dialogue are read while standing obliquely (not directly) behind their Characters. The Shadow may also reach from behind and adjust the physical condition of the Character, just as though Shadow and Character shared one body.

Simple properties and costume pieces may help the Characters feel their roles. A crown for Herod, a length of purple fabric for Jesus' robe, some silver shields made from large pizza cardboards for the soldiers are examples of how to suggest roles and would satisfy the need for a costume while performing a play. The only necessary property is a cross for Jesus and Simon of Cyrene. Much of the rest can be left to the imagination.

Look carefully at both these instructions and the script itself. You will see much that will help you effectively combine persons of differing abilities in meaningful interaction with Scripture. The format presupposes a traditional sanctuary: a long central aisle and a raised chancel. If your sanctuary is different, you will need to make some changes.

In general, the action should precede the words, thus avoiding the trite, "stagy" affect of much amateur drama.

Cast of Characters and Their Shadows

High Priest
Jesus
Pilate
Priest I
Priest II
Herod
Soldiers
Officer
Simon of Cyrene
Woman
Penitent Thief
Impenitent Thief
Extras: Council Members, Women of Jerusalem,
Women Followers of Jesus, Citizens

Note: Although it is possible to do this reading with as few as three persons, the object here is to involve as many persons as possible.

[Vs. 1] At curtain's rise High Priest and Council Members are seated in choir stalls. Jesus is positioned at center stage. High Priest takes Jesus by the elbow. Remember that each Character has a Shadow and only the Shadow speaks. The Character and Shadow move together as much as possible, with the Character in the foreground, and the Shadow as visually inconspicuous as possible.

HIGH PRIEST
The Council rose up and took
Jesus before Pilate.

The High Priest and Council members exit with Jesus through a side door and re-enter at the foot of the chancel steps. Pilate meets them and stands above them at the top of the chancel steps. [Vs. 2] The High Priest stretches out his arm pointing toward Jesus accusingly.

HIGH PRIEST
(to congregation) They began to
accuse him. *(to Pilate)* We caught
this man misleading our people.

PRIEST I
*(imitates High Priest's accusing
gesture)* Telling them not to pay
taxes to the Emperor . . .

PRIEST II
*(joins the other accusers in pointing
to Jesus)* . . . And claiming that he
himself is the Messiah, a king.

*[Vs. 3] Pilate studies Jesus' face. Jesus maintains eye
contact.*

PILATE
Are you the King of the Jews?

JESUS
So you say.

*[Vs. 4] Pilate stares back at Jesus, then crosses to lectern,
raises both arms like a politician addressing a large
assembly.*

PILATE
(to congregation) Then Pilate said
to the chief priests and the crowds
(to the High Priest and Council),
"I find no reason to condemn this man."

*[Vs. 5] High Priest, Priest I. Priest II and Council raise
clenched fists.*

HIGH PRIEST
With his teaching he is starting a
riot among the people all through
Judea.

PRIEST I
He began in Galilee.

Pilate starts at the word "Galilee" and looks sharply from Priest I to Jesus.

PRIEST II
And now he has come here.

[Vs. 6] Pilate studies faces of Council Members.

PILATE
Is this man a Galilean?

COUNCIL MEMBERS
(ad lib) He is! Yes, a Galilean!
That's right - from Galilee. *(etc.)*

[Vs. 7] While Pilate and Council are speaking, Soldiers move a large throne-like chair into chancel opposite Pilate. Herod sits on his throne.

PILATE
When he learned that Jesus was from
the region ruled by Herod, he sent
him to Herod.

HEROD
Herod was also in Jerusalem at that
time.

Council redirects its attention to Herod. They push Jesus before Herod's throne. [Vs. 8] Herod leans toward Jesus and rubs his hands together in a greedy, hungry manner grinning like "a sly fox."

HEROD
Herod was very pleased when he saw Jesus because he had heard about him and had been wanting to see him for a long time. He was hoping to see Jesus perform some miracle.

[Vs. 9] Herod sits back on his throne in affected relaxation. He looks out over the heads of all as though thinking to himself, waves a hand casually, perhaps studies his fingernails, as he tries to pose difficult questions to Jesus.

HEROD
So Herod asked Jesus many questions.

Herod extends an arm in invitation. Jesus turns away and looks off into the distance. Herod repeats his invitation, this time more brusquely. He balls his hand into a fist and beats on the arm of his throne.

JESUS
But Jesus made no answer.

[Vs. 10] Council Members repeat accusatory gesture. High Priest, Priest I and Priest II take up the gesture as well.

HIGH PRIEST
The chief priests and the teachers of
the Law stepped forward and made
strong accusations against Jesus.

[Vs. 11] Herod lolls on his throne. He gives Jesus a dismissive wave of his hand. He turns toward Soldiers and "speaks" behind the back of his hand in an aside. Soldiers, Council and Herod laugh mockingly.

HEROD
Herod and his soldiers made fun of
Jesus and treated him with contempt.

Soldiers wrap purple fabric around Jesus' shoulders. They shove Jesus to the other side of the chancel where Pilate stands waiting.

OFFICER
They put a fine robe on him and
sent him back to Pilate.

[Vs. 12] Herod rises. Soldiers remove throne. Herod turns and bows conspiratorially toward Pilate. Pilate returns the bow. They understand one another perfectly.

HEROD

On that very day Herod and Pilate
became friends. *(Herod and soldiers
exit.)*

PILATE

Before, they had been enemies.

*[Vs. 13]   Pilate returns to lectern for another public
statement. He is tense. His hands grip the lectern authori-
tatively.*

PILATE

Pilate called together the chief
priests, the leaders and the people
and said to them *[vs. 14]*, "You
brought this man to me and said
that he was misleading the people.
Now I have examined him here in
your presence, and I have not found
him guilty of any of the crimes you
accuse him of."

*[Vs. 15] Pilate indicates the opposite side of the chancel
where Herod's throne had been.*

PILATE

Nor did Herod find him guilty, for he
sent him back to us. There is nothing
this man has done to deserve death.

[Vs. 16] Pilate raises his hand as though pronouncing official sentence upon Jesus.

PILATE
So I will have him whipped and
let him go.

[Vs. 18] Council raise and lower angry fists as though in time to chanting "Kill him! Kill him!"

HIGH PRIEST
The whole crowd cried out,
"Kill him!"

PRIEST I
Set Barabbas free for us!

PRIEST II
[Vs. 19] Barabbas had been put
in prison for a riot that had taken
place in the city . . .

PRIEST I
. . . and for murder.

[Vs. 20] Pilate runs his hands through his hair in frustration and then extends both arms with hands up in appeal.

PILATE
Pilate wanted to set Jesus free so
he appealed to the crowd again.

PRIEST I
[Vs. 21] Crucify him!

PRIEST II
Crucify him!

*[Vs. 22] Pilate reaches out toward various members of the
Council, pleading with them.*

PILATE
Pilate said to them a third time,
"But what crime has he committed?
I cannot find he has done anything
to deserve death! I will have him
whipped and set him free."

*[Vs. 23] Council repeats gesture of raising and lowering
clenched fists, this time in rhythm to the chant, "Crucify him!
Crucify him!" They may mouth the words.*

HIGH PRIEST
But they kept on shouting at the
top of their voices that Jesus
should be crucified.

Pilate grips lectern as though to steady himself. His shoulders slump. His body says failure and defeat.

> PILATE
> And finally their shouting succeeded.
> *[Vs. 24]* So Pilate passed the sentence
> on Jesus that they were asking for.
> *[Vs. 25]* He set free the man they
> wanted, the one who had been put in
> prison for riot and murder.

Pilate gestures toward Jesus and looks for Jesus' forgiveness.

> PILATE
> And he handed Jesus over for them
> to do as they wished.

Pilate exits slowly. His shoulders sag under the weight of sacrificing his integrity to public pressure.

[Vs. 26] The Women of Jerusalem and the Citizens enter and line the center aisle. They may crouch, sit, or half kneel so as not to obscure the sightlines. As Jesus passes, they reach out with challenges, comfort, requests and prayers. Soldiers enter carrying the cross, which they put on Jesus' back. Jesus staggers under the weight.

> OFFICER
> The soldiers led Jesus away . . .

Soldiers, Officer and Jesus begin slow exit down center aisle toward narthex. Simon of Cyrene enters from rear of sanctuary heading toward the chancel. All meet about one quarter of the way down the aisle.

OFFICER
They met a men . . .

SIMON OF CYRENE
. . . from Cyrene named Simon who was coming into the city from the country.

Soldiers grab Simon of Cyrene and take the cross from Jesus and put it on Simon. Soldiers shove Jesus forward, with Simon following after.

OFFICER
They seized him . . .

SIMON OF CYRENE
. . . put the cross on him and made him carry it behind Jesus.

WOMAN
[Vs. 27] A large crowd of people followed him; among them were some women who were weeping and wailing for him.

[Vs. 28] Jesus focuses first on one woman and then on another.

JESUS

Jesus turned to them and said,
"Women of Jerusalem! Don't cry
for me, but for yourselves and for
your children. *[Vs. 29]* For the
days are coming when people will
say, 'How lucky are the women who
never had children, who never bore
babies, who never nursed them!'
[vs. 30] That will be the time when
people will say to the mountains,
'Fall on us!' and to the hills, 'Hide us!'
For if such things happen when the wood
is green, what will happen when it is dry?"

All exit down center aisle. The soldiers, Jesus and Simon of Cyrene are in the front of the procession. The Women of Jerusalem and the Citizens fall in behind as the main group passes. All reconvene as quickly as possible at the chancel steps. The Penitent Thief and the Impenitent Thief enter and stand on Jesus' right and left, one step lower. Jesus is at center. Jesus, the Penitent Thief and the Impenitent Thief may hold poles across their shoulders to support their arms in an attitude of crucifixion. [Vs. 32]

IMPENITENT THIEF

Two other men. . .

PENITENT THIEF
. . . both of them criminals . . .

IMPENITENT THIEF
were also led out to be put to death
with Jesus. *[Vs. 33]*

OFFICER
When they came to the place called
"The Skull," they crucified Jesus there
and the two criminals.

PENITENT THIEF
One on his right. . .

IMPENITENT THIEF
and the other on his left.

*[Vs. 34]   Jesus slowly looks into the faces of the
crowd—including the congregation.   At last he looks up to
heaven.*

JESUS
Forgive them, Father! They don't know
what they are doing.

*Soldiers mime throwing dice.   They have a tug-of-war over
the purple cloak.*

OFFICER
They divided his clothes among
themselves by throwing dice.

WOMAN
[Vs. 35] The people stood there
watching.

HIGH PRIEST
While their leaders made fun of him.

PRIEST I
He saved others!

PRIEST II
Let him save himself!

HIGH PRIEST
If he is the Messiah whom God
has chosen.

*[Vs. 36] Soldiers mime carrying wineskin, bowing servilely
and offering Jesus a drink.*

OFFICER
The soldiers also made fun of him;
they came up to him and offered
cheap wine and said *(changes voice
to gruffer, more gravelly sound)*,

OFFICER *(continued)*
"Save yourself if you are the King
of the Jews!"

JESUS
[Vs. 38] Above him were written
these words: This is the King of the
Jews!

[Vs. 39] Impenitent Thief sneers and jeers at Jesus.

IMPENITENT THIEF
One of the criminals hanging there
hurled insults at him: aren't you the
Messiah? Save yourself and us.

*[Vs. 40] Penitent Thief jerks his head up, suddenly alert. He
turns his head toward Jesus and then looks back at the
Impenitent Thief.*

PENITENT THIEF
The other one, however, rebuked
him saying, "Don't you fear God?
You received the same sentence he
did. *[Vs. 41]* Ours, however, is only
right, because we are getting what
we deserve for what we did, but he
has done no wrong. *([Vs. 42] He
looks yearningly toward Jesus.)*

PENITENT THIEF
(continued)
Remember me, Jesus, when you
come as King!"

JESUS
[Vs. 43] I promise you that today
you will be in paradise with me.

WOMAN
[Vs. 44] It was about twelve o'clock
when the sun stopped shining, and
darkness covered the whole country
until three o'clock.

HIGH PRIEST
[Vs. 45] The curtain hanging in the
Temple was torn in two.

[Vs. 46] Jesus raises his head to look heavenward.

JESUS
Jesus cried out in a loud voice,
"Father! In your hands I place my
spirit." *(Jesus drops his head to his
chest.)* He said this and died.

*[Vs. 47] Officer puts one foot on lowest chancel step. He
leans in looking at Jesus with awe, then bows his head.*

OFFICER

The army officer saw what had
happened, and he praised God saying,
"Certainly he was a good man!"

*[Vs. 48] Council and Citizens exit slowly, shaking their heads
in confusion.*

WOMAN

When the people who had gathered
there to watch the spectacle saw what
happened, they all went back home,
beating their breasts in sorrow.

*[Vs. 49] The Women of Jerusalem lean on one another's
shoulders. Some cry, and others comfort those who weep.*

WOMAN

All those who knew Jesus personally,
including the women who had
followed him from Galilee, stood at
a distance to watch.

*With the help of their Shadows, the Penitent Thief, the
Impenitent Thief and Jesus disengage their arms from the
poles and exit. The Soldiers exit. The Women of Jerusalem
exit opposite the Soldiers.*

Silence.

Lo-Ann and David Trembley are founding co-pastors of Broken Walls Christian Community, an inner-city congregation in Milwaukee, Wisconsin. The church's name comes from Ephesians 2:14: "The dividing walls of hostility have all been broken down." The congregation's mission statement is to be fully inclusive. The ethnic make-up is one-third Hispanic, one-third African American, and one-third Anglo. Services are held in both Spanish and English, and there is a significant contingent of persons who happen to be mentally challenged.

The Trembleys are co-authors of the five-booklet "Drama in the Church" series, published by Educational Ministries, Prescott, Arizona (1994-95). They have substantial experience serving as keynote speakers and workshop leaders at church-growth, evangelism, worship and Christian education conferences.

Lo-Ann is a professional storyteller, dramatic artist and musician. She is associated with Center for Strings, a consortium of women who teach violin, viola and cello. She plays with the recorder consort Mystic Winds and is their arranger. Her academic credentials include a B. A., cum laude, in Theatre (University of Toledo [Ohio], 1974), an M. Div. (Chicago Theological Seminary; 1978) and an M.A. in Theatre and Interpersonal Communication (Marquette University: Milwaukee, Wisconsin, 1990).

David teaches writing at Milwaukee Area Technical College and is a member of the Wisconsin Fellowship of Poets. He also owns a communications counseling service that specializes in meeting the needs of small businesses and non-profit organizations. His academic credentials include a B.S. in Education (Indiana University: Bloomington, IN, 1966), an M. Div. (Chicago Theological Seminary, 1977) and graduate work in education from the University of Wisconsin-Milwaukee.

The Trembleys are currently at work on three new books. *Sensing God*, an account of how to get in touch (and sight, smell, hearing, and taste) with God. *Spiritual Explorations for Families with Preschoolers* is a resource for doing family devotions. *Being Church in the Post-Christian Age* shares the vision of Broken Walls as a model of how the Church might re-form itself in a thoroughly secular world.